PRIMARY SOURCES IN AMERICAN HISTORY™

THE LEWIS AND CLARK EXPEDITION
A PRIMARY SOURCE HISTORY OF THE JOURNEY OF THE CORPS OF DISCOVERY

TAMRA ORR

rosen central

Primary Source™

The Rosen Publishing Group, Inc., New York

Published in 2004 by The Rosen Publishing Group, Inc.
29 East 21st Street, New York, NY 10010

First Edition

Library of Congress Cataloging-in-Publication Data

Orr, Tamra.
The Lewis and Clark Expedition : a primary source history of the journey of the Corps of Discovery / Tamra Orr.— 1st ed.
    p. cm. — (Primary sources in American history)
Summary: Examines the events and key figures behind the incredibly adventurous and treacherous exploration of the United States' western frontier.
Includes bibliographical references and index.
ISBN 0-8239-4005-5 (lib. bdg.)
1. Lewis and Clark Expedition (1804–1806)—Juvenile literature. 2. Lewis and Clark Expedition (1804–1806)—Sources—Juvenile literature. 3. Lewis, Meriwether, 1774–1809—Juvenile literature. 4. Clark, William, 1770–1838—Juvenile literature. 5. West (U.S.)—Discovery and exploration—Juvenile literature. 6. West (U.S.)—Discovery and exploration—Sources—Juvenile literature. [1. Lewis and Clark Expedition (1804–1806) 2. Lewis, Meriwether, 1774–1809. 3. Clark, William, 1770–1838. 4. West (U.S.)—Discovery and exploration.]
I. Title. II. Series.
F592.7.O69 2004
917.804'2—dc21

2002156100

Manufactured in the United States of America

On the front cover: *Lewis and Clark in Council with Indians*, an engraving c. 1812 by Patrick Gass. Courtesy of the Rare Book and Special Collections Division of the Library of Congress.

On the back cover: First row (left to right): immigrants arriving at Ellis Island; Generals Lee and Grant meet to discuss terms of Confederate surrender at Appomattox, Virginia. Second row (left to right): Lewis and Clark meeting with a western Native American tribe during the expedition of the Corps of Discovery; Napoléon at the signing of the Louisiana Purchase. Third row (left to right): Cherokees traveling along the Trail of Tears during their forced relocation west of the Mississippi River; escaped slaves traveling on the Underground Railroad.

CONTENTS

INTRODUCTION

JEFFERSON'S AMERICAN DREAM

When Thomas Jefferson was elected president in 1800, the United States was a very young country—and a much smaller one. Encompassing a mere seventeen states—from the Atlantic Ocean west to the Mississippi River—the nation was only about a quarter of the size it is today. Two-thirds of its five million people lived within fifty miles of the Atlantic Ocean. Spain, England, and France claimed other parts of the largely unexplored continent. European control over the land and trade of any part of the continent angered Jefferson. He dreamed of a United States that would someday stretch from the Atlantic Ocean to encompass all that lay between its current western boundary—the Mississippi River—and the distant, mighty Pacific Ocean.

The foreign land spreading hundreds and hundreds of miles beyond the young nation's western border—so close, yet so forbidding—was an intriguing mystery. What lay beyond the Mississippi River? What types of animals, plants, and people could be found there? Where did the rivers lead? How could the vast lands be explored and then made part of this new country?

These questions preoccupied Jefferson for nearly twenty years before he was elected president. Twice before, he had tried

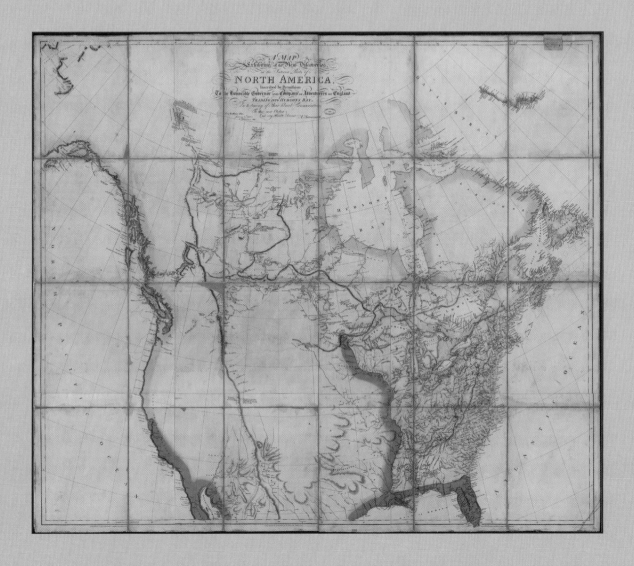

When Lewis and Clark set off on their expedition to explore the western lands the United States had recently acquired through the Louisiana Purchase, they brought along this 1802 map created by the cartographer Aaron Arrowsmith. The lack of information on the western "wilderness" is apparent in the map's lack of detail west of the Mississippi River. One of Lewis and Clark's main duties on their expedition was to draw detailed and precise maps of the country's vast new territory.

to send explorers out to investigate and study these unknown lands, but his efforts failed. As president, however, Jefferson now had the necessary power and influence to organize a group of adventurers who could finally explore the mysteries of the western frontier. Through a combination of burning curiosity and political insight, he made a decision that drastically changed the face of the nation and inspired the people of the United States to look westward to their—and their nation's—future.

As Jefferson was considering how to explore the land to the west, the political situation in Europe was changing rapidly. These changes had a dramatic effect on the North American territory held by European powers. In 1762, Spain acquired from France the western portion of an enormous but unprofitable block of North American land called the Louisiana Territory. (The following year, France gave the portion of the Louisiana Territory lying east of the Mississippi to Great Britain.) The 828,000-square-mile (just over two million square kilometers) western section stretched from the Gulf of Mexico to the upper region of present-day Montana and from the Mississippi River to the present-day borders of Montana and Idaho. In 1800, however, Spain signed the Treaty of San Ildefonso with France. This treaty returned the Louisiana Territory to France and its emperor, Napoléon Bonaparte.

Jefferson was worried that France, having regained possession of the Louisiana Territory, would threaten America's western borders and deny the United States access to the port of New Orleans at the mouth of the Mississippi River. This port was vital to U.S. trade at the time and needed to be protected and kept open at all costs. In an effort to save the port, Jefferson sent Robert Livingston, his minister to France, and James Monroe, future president and then governor of Virginia, to Paris

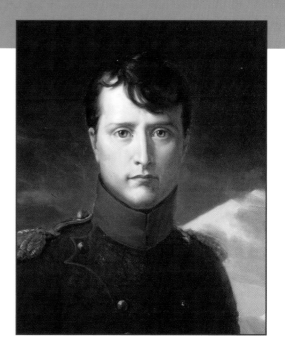

Thomas Jefferson *(left)* was inaugurated president of the United States in 1801. Napoléon Bonaparte *(right)* was declared emperor of France in 1804. The two men rose to power at almost the same time, and they shared a common enemy—England. Jefferson did not admire Napoléon, whom he considered a tyrant, but he benefited greatly from Napoléon's conflict with England. In need of money to wage war against the English, Napoléon decided to sell the Louisiana Territory to the United States. As a result, not only did the United States double in size overnight, it was also able to expand and grow strong without interference while England's army and navy were distracted by Napoléon's forces.

to discuss with Napoléon the possibility of the United States buying New Orleans. The men were authorized to offer up to $9.375 million for it.

When Livingston and Monroe met with Bonaparte's spokesperson, Maurice de Talleyrand, they had no idea that they were about to be the recipients of an amazing stroke of good fortune. In fact, their mission seemed doomed to failure at first. The initial offer by the United States to purchase New Orleans was refused. Days later, however, that decision was reversed in dramatic fashion.

This is a map of North America from 1803, created by John Luffman. Luffman was an accomplished engraver, mapmaker, and publisher based in London, England, who specialized in European subjects. Based on the scant information available, the map's rendering of the land west of the Mississippi River is not entirely accurate. It does provide a good sense, however, of the vast size of the Louisiana Territory (the pink central portion) and the valuable addition it represented to the United States. One of the results of the Lewis and Clark expedition was the creation of an extremely accurate and detailed map of the United States's western lands.

Napoléon, concerned about raising enough money for a war he was planning against Great Britain, made a counteroffer. To the great surprise and delight of Livingston and Monroe, he offered to sell New Orleans to the United States, but only if the Americans also agreed to purchase the entire Louisiana Territory. Monroe and Livingston were shocked; they had never dreamed that an offer like this one would be made. In addition to raising money for his military efforts in Europe, Napoléon, knowing he would never be able to defend this large territory against the inevitable encroachment of Americans, instead hoped to shift the balance of power in Europe by selling the territory. By acquiring the Louisiana Territory, the United States, a fellow enemy of Great Britain, would be greatly strengthened and would provide a useful challenge to British dominance in both the Old and New Worlds.

Monroe and Livingston could not discuss the offer with Jefferson because it would take weeks to get a message to him across the Atlantic, let alone a reply. They were forced to make an enormously important decision on their own. After a brief round of negotiations, they agreed to buy the 828,000 square miles (2,145,000 sq. km) of territory for $15 million—averaging about three cents per acre. The size of the United States was almost doubled when the treaty that formalized the Louisiana Purchase was signed on April 30, 1803. The door was now open to what would become one of the greatest expeditions in history. First conceived by Jefferson as a secretive survey of foreign land, it was now suddenly transformed into a triumphant survey of American land.

Despite drawing criticism from some members of Congress, the press, and the public regarding the Louisiana Purchase, Jefferson held firm and went ahead with plans to explore the new American territory. Critics believed that far too much money had been spent to acquire a vast wasteland that would never be productive or populated. Few people at the time could envision how rich in resources and fertile this new land was, nor could they anticipate the country's future population growth and increasing need for space and desire to control the continent.

On January 18, 1803, before the Louisiana Purchase was officially completed, Jefferson sent Congress a secret message

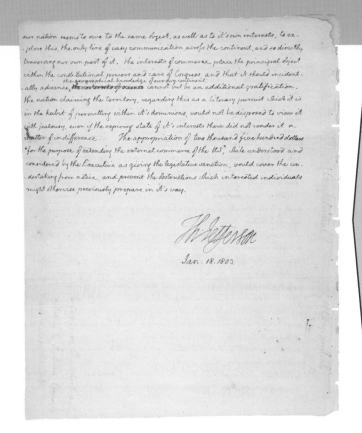

our nation seems to owe to the same object, as well as to it's own interests, to explore this, the only line of easy communication across the continent, and so directly traversing our own part of it. the interests of commerce place the principal object within the constitutional powers and care of Congress, and that it should incidentally advance the geographical knowledge of our own continent, cannot but be an additional gratification. the nation claiming the territory, regarding this as a literary pursuit which it is in the habit of permitting within it's dominions, would not be disposed to view it with jealousy, even if the exploring state of it's interests there did not render it a matter of indifference. the appropriation of two thousand five hundred dollars "for the purpose of extending the external commerce of the US", while understood and considered by the Executive as giving the legislative sanction, would cover the undertaking from notice, and prevent the distractions which interested individuals might otherwise previously prepare in it's way.

Th. Jefferson

Jan. 18. 1803.

requesting the $2,500 he would need to fund the expedition to the West (actual costs would reach $38,722 by the time the expedition came to an end). In an effort to persuade Congress of the practical value of the expedition, Jefferson claimed its main purpose was to promote and improve trade. In a letter to Congress (now housed in the National Archives), he wrote, "The river Missouri and the Indians inhabiting it, are not as well known as is rendered desirable by their connection with the Mississippi, and consequently with us." He then proposed that an "intelligent officer with ten or twelve chosen men . . . might explore the whole line, even to the Western Ocean." The aim of these adventurous men would be "to make friends and allies of the far Western Indians while at the same time diverting valuable pelts from the rugged northern routes used by another nation [Great Britain] . . . and bringing the harvest down the Missouri to the Mississippi and thence eastward by a variety of routes."

A month later, the request was approved. Jefferson wanted the expedition to accomplish several different objectives. The first was political and diplomatic in nature. He would send his explorers out to establish the country's ownership of its new territory. The corps of explorers would notify any Europeans and Indians they encountered of the Louisiana Purchase and the recent change in the land's ownership. Friendly relations with the various Native American nations were to be fostered to promote peace in the new lands.

Developing new trade possibilities with the Indian nations was another important objective of the expedition. Jefferson hoped to convince the Indians to begin trading with only the United States, not Britain. In addition, he hoped that his explorers would discover the fabled Northwest Passage, a water route that would connect various rivers, cross the western mountains, and empty out into the Pacific Ocean. A transcontinental water route would increase the volume of goods, such as fur pelts, that could be shipped back east and sold to U.S. and European markets.

The third objective of the trip would satisfy Jefferson's keen interest in science. He was as eager to find out about the plants, animals, and geography of the West as he was to establish communication and trade with the Indians. His library in Monticello is thought to have contained the largest collection of books on the western lands in the world. In a June 20, 1803, letter to Meriwether Lewis, Jefferson directed his corps of explorers to make a careful study of the Indians, their languages and customs, and "the soil and face of the country, its growth and vegetable productions . . . the animals of the country generally and especially those not known in the United States" (quoted in Donald Jackson's *Letters of the Lewis and*

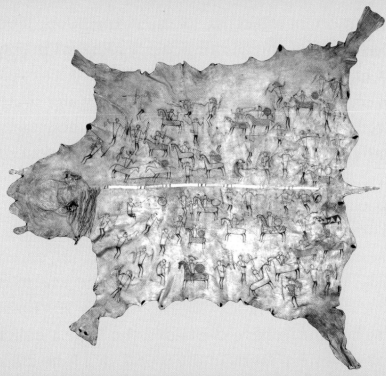

President Jefferson's library at Monticello *(top)*, his estate near Charlottesville, Virginia, was said to include the largest collection of reference works on the western lands of North America. His scientific interest in the West was great, so he encouraged Lewis and Clark to keep detailed records of their observations and send back as many specimens and artifacts as they could. One of the artifacts he received was a buffalo robe *(below)* painted by a man from the Mandan tribe with a scene from an eight-year-old battle between the Lakota Sioux and the Mandan.

Clark Expedition). Jefferson also wanted his team of explorers to measure the latitude and longitude of the land to help determine the position of the tributaries (smaller streams that feed a river) of the Missouri River and the actual borders of the Louisiana Territory, which were not precisely known.

The only question remaining was, Who would lead this incredible journey? Ever since Jefferson conceived of this particular western exploratory expedition, he had wanted it to be led by Meriwether Lewis, his private secretary and old family friend. He had known him personally for years and was confident in his skills and abilities as a soldier, diplomat, and naturalist. In turn, Lewis would select his friend William Clark—a fellow soldier and wilderness trekker—to go with him and share leadership duties.

The plans were finalized, the stage was set, and the players were ready. One of the most unforgettable expeditions in the history of the United States was about to begin—the amazing journey of Lewis and Clark and the Corps of Discovery.

TIMELINE

1770	William Clark is born.
1774	Meriwether Lewis is born.
1775	The Revolutionary War begins.
1776	The Continental Congress adopts the Declaration of Independence in Philadelphia, Pennsylvania.
1783	Revolutionary War officially ends with the signing of the Paris Peace Treaty.
1800	Thomas Jefferson is elected president.
1801	Lewis becomes Jefferson's private secretary.
1802	Lewis is asked to command the expedition to explore the West.
1803	The Louisiana Purchase is made. Lewis asks Clark to join him on the exploratory expedition.
1804	Jefferson is reelected. The Corps of Discovery sets out from St. Louis, reaches Mandan villages, and makes a winter camp.

TIMELINE

1805 —— The expedition crosses the Continental Divide and follows the Columbia River to the Pacific Ocean, then winters at Fort Clatsop.

1806 —— Lewis and Clark separate to recross the Continental Divide, then join at the mouth of the Yellowstone River, reaching St. Louis again in September.

1807 —— Lewis is appointed governor of Louisiana Territory. Clark is appointed brigadier general of the militia and superintendent of Indian Affairs for the Territory of Upper Louisiana.

1809 —— Lewis dies.

1813 —— Clark is appointed governor of Missouri Territory.

1814 —— The journals of Lewis and Clark are published.

1826 —— Jefferson dies.

1838 —— Clark dies.

CHAPTER 1

In addition to personally planning many details of the upcoming expedition, Jefferson also handpicked the leader of the mission: Meriwether Lewis, his private secretary and son of Jefferson family friends William and Lucy Meriwether Lewis.

THE CORPS OF DISCOVERY

Lewis was a handsome man of six feet (well above the average for men at that time). He was slim, quiet, and serious. His mother had been a local herb doctor and taught him most of what he knew about health and medicine. His years spent in the woods behind his family's home taught him important lessons about wildlife and hunting, which would be invaluable on the expedition.

Meriwether Lewis

Lewis was only thirty years old when the expedition set out, but he had already handled a great deal of responsibility in his short life. By his mid-twenties, he had taken over the management of his family's farm, Locust Hill, to help his twice-widowed mother and siblings. He had joined the militia during the Whiskey Rebellion of 1794 (a rebellion of western Pennsylvania farmers angered by a tax upon whiskey that cut into their wheat profits). While still in his twenties, Lewis was also assigned to a rifle company in Fort Greenville, Ohio, where he met William Clark and served under him. By age twenty-six, he had reached the rank of captain.

Meriwether Lewis—pictured above in an 1807 portrait by Charles Willson Peale—was born into a Virginia plantation family in 1774, two years before the start of the American Revolution. Lewis would begin his military career in 1794 with the Virginia Militia and eventually rose to the rank of captain in the U.S. Army in 1801. When family friend Thomas Jefferson first considered an expedition to explore the West in 1792, Lewis immediately volunteered but was considered too young and inexperienced to be qualified.

Locust Hill was located near Thomas Jefferson's family home, Monticello, and the two families had known each other for years. Jefferson had watched Lewis grow up to be an intelligent, responsible, and skilled man. He asked Lewis to be his secretary as soon as he was elected president, and in the following months, Lewis was a frequent visitor to Monticello.

The president was quietly preparing Lewis for the upcoming journey by encouraging him to read the many books he had in his library, including those on botany, medicine, navigation, cartography, astronomy, and geology. In addition to these studies, Lewis was sent to Philadelphia to be tutored by a variety of experts. Physician Benjamin Rush taught him the basics of practicing medicine. Astronomer Andrew Ellicott taught him how to navigate a boat by looking at constellations. And Benjamin Smith Barton, professor of botany, taught him how to identify and scientifically describe plants.

William Clark

In 1975, when Lewis met William Clark at Fort Greenville, Ohio, they quickly became friends. Clark was four years older than Lewis and was the ninth of ten children by John and Ann Clark. His early years were spent in Virginia and Kentucky. At age nineteen, he joined the militia as his older brothers had done. By 1795, he was a captain in the regular army. During his time as a soldier, he learned about commanding men, drawing maps, and building forts—all skills that would assist him in the future. In 1796, Clark retired from the military and returned to Kentucky to run his family farm, Mulberry Hill.

Like Meriwether Lewis, Clark was a tall man of six feet. His appearance was even more striking because of his brilliant red hair. Unlike his partner, however, Clark was outgoing and talkative. He loved adventure and hoped to do something more exciting

William Clark—pictured above in an 1807 Charles Willson Peale portrait—was born into a Virginia plantation family in 1770. Clark joined the frontier militia as a young man and became an officer in the U.S. Army in 1792, but he resigned his commission to run the family plantation in Kentucky. Lewis, a fellow officer who served under Clark, would "rescue" him from a sedate farmer's life he did not want by inviting him to cocaptain the Corps of Discovery's adventurous expedition.

with his life than simply run the family farm of nine thousand acres. His good friend Lewis was about to offer him the opportunity to do exactly that.

On June 19, 1803, Lewis wrote a letter to his friend Clark to tell him of his upcoming adventure and to ask if he would be interested in serving as cocaptain. He wrote, in the often haphazard spelling and grammar of the day, "My friend . . . if there is anything in this enterprise which would induce you to participate with me in it's fatiegues, it's dangers and it's honors, believe me, there is no man on earth with whom I should feel equal in sharing them as with yourself" (as quoted in Christine A. Fitzgerald's *The World's Great Explorers*).

Clark was so thrilled when he received the letter that he responded the next day, saying, "This is an undertaking fraited with many difeculties, but My friend I do assure you that no man lives whith whome I would perfur to undertake Such a Trip as yourself. My friend, I join you with hand and Heart" (as quoted in George Sullivan's *Lewis and Clark: In Their Own Words*).

The Preparations

Anyone who has ever packed to go on a trip knows that it requires a lot of thought and preparation. When that trip is going to last at least two years and extend into mysterious places where the weather, temperature, and terrain are unknown and supplies must be sufficient for dozens of hardworking, hungry men, preparation is more than a chore—it is a tremendously challenging undertaking in its own right.

Lewis had already been preparing for his journey for almost two years before he asked Clark to join the expedition. In addition to gaining a rapid education in a wide variety of fields—such as botany, cartography, and medicine—Lewis also focused

This is a supply list handwritten by Meriwether Lewis detailing some of the goods and equipment that the Corps of Discovery would need to successfully complete and survive their two-year expedition. This portion of the list is broken down into three categories—arms and accoutrements, ammunition, and clothing. Some of the items include rifles, gunpowder, bullet molds, blankets, shirts, and socks. Congress had authorized Lewis and Clark to spend $2,500 for the entire expedition. Actual costs would balloon to almost $40,000. See transcript on pages 57–58.

on the trip's practical requirements. Two days after the Louisiana Purchase was first publicly announced on July 3, 1803, Lewis left Washington, D.C., for Pittsburgh, Pennsylvania, to begin purchasing supplies and hiring men for the expedition.

Initially authorized to spend $2,500, he compiled list after list of what would be needed, from medical supplies and food to clothing and weapons. These lists offer great insight into the wide variety of situations expected for an expedition of this scope and duration. Scientific equipment, camping supplies, presents for the Native Americans, weapons, clothing, and food added up to almost two tons of materials that would need to be hauled along on the trip.

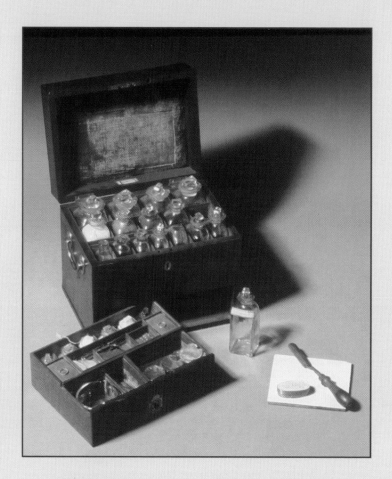

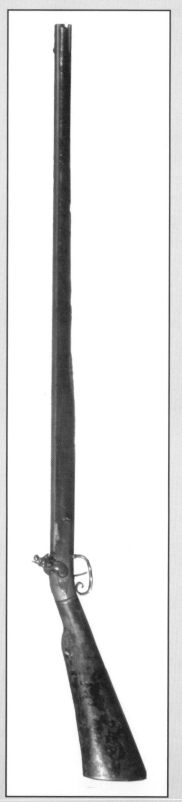

Lewis invested in the most up-to-date equipment of the day to help him in drawing maps and taking measurements. Compasses, quadrants (for measuring altitude), telescopes, and chronometers (for calculating longitude) were put on the list. Camp supplies came next, including 150 yards of cloth for making tents and sheets, pliers, hatchets, saws, fishing hooks and lines, cooking utensils, mosquito netting, knapsacks, and twelve pounds of soap. Dr. Rush put together a medicine kit with bandages and surgical instruments for the journey. Clothing for all the men included nearly four dozen flannel shirts, coats, shoes, blankets, stockings, and pants. More than 400 pounds of sheet lead were bought for making bullets, along with 176 pounds of gunpowder packed in 52 lead canisters, numerous knives, and more than a dozen rifles.

Food was another vitally important supply. Other explorers had not been able to make the same trek because they had run out of food. Lewis was determined this would not happen to his group. While much of the food they ate would come from the wildlife they hunted on the trail, he also bought staples such as ground corn, 3,400 pounds of flour, 3 bushels of salt, 50 kegs of salt pork, 600 barrels of grease, and 193 pounds of "portable

This is some of the equipment brought on the expedition by the Corps of Discovery. At top left is a medicine kit owned by Dr. Benjamin Rush similar to the one he put together for Lewis, who served as the corps' medic. At bottom left is Clark's compass used to help him determine direction and calculate longitude and latitude. Measurements taken with this instrument would help him create his detailed map of the American West. Rifles were also given to corps members for the purposes of hunting and self-defense. The gun at right is Lewis's own air rifle, purchased especially for the expedition.

soup" (in 32 canisters), which was a paste of boiled beef, eggs, and vegetables that needed only water to be complete.

Because the land Lewis and Clark would be traversing was mostly unexplored by Americans and Europeans and because they were relatively new to the formal study of science, they also needed to carry a small reference library with them. These materials included handbooks on botany, mineralogy, and astronomy; a history of the Louisiana Territory; maps of portions of the Missouri River; and tables to help determine longitude and latitude.

And, finally, Lewis purchased presents to trade with the Native Americans. A good portion of his job on this expedition was to study the different tribes and report back vital information such as their locations, languages, clothing, shelters, customs, and religions. To help smooth the way for their first encounters and build trust for future peaceful relations, Lewis bought items he hoped the Native Americans would like. These included pocket mirrors, combs, ribbons, handkerchiefs, sewing needles and thread, kettles, tobacco, knives, beads, brightly dyed cloths, and face paint. Two special gifts prepared especially for this trip were Jefferson's peace medals and certificates of greeting. The silver medals had "Peace and Friendship" engraved upon them and featured an image of the president. Lewis and Clark also handed out certificates bearing Jefferson's personal greetings to show the kindness of the "Great White Father" living in Washington, D.C.

After Clark accepted Lewis's offer to join the expedition, he traveled to Clarksville, Indiana Territory (just opposite Louisville), to begin organizing the expedition and recruiting men while Lewis went to Pittsburgh to prepare the boats and supplies needed for the long trip ahead. The approximately four dozen men eventually chosen for the trip came from a wide

When these chiefs of the Omaha, Kansas, Missouri, Oto, and Pawnee Indians visited Washington, D.C., in 1821, the artist Charles Bird King painted their portrait. The second figure from the left wears one of Jefferson's peace medals around his neck (both sides of a replica medal are shown at right). Jefferson was not the first president to issue peace medals. The tradition actually began with George Washington. Never before, however, had the medals been distributed so far west, to previously unknown tribes in unexplored lands. Any Indian who accepted a peace medal from Lewis and Clark was expected to remain loyal to his or her "Great White Father" and the United States, especially in any conflict with the continent's other, European powers—the British, the French, and the Spanish.

variety of places and backgrounds (the exact number of corps members is unknown). Some were Kentucky woodsmen, some were soldiers, and others were hunters or scouts. There were men from Virginia, Kentucky, New Hampshire, and Pennsylvania, as well as some from as far away as Canada and Germany. Most were young, single, healthy, and strong. They

This is a roster of the men who signed on to the Corps of Discovery, handwritten by William Clark. The first four names on the list are the corps' sergeants—John Ordway, Nathaniel Pryor, Charles Floyd (who would be the first U.S. soldier to die west of the Mississippi River), and Patrick Gass. Gass, a skilled artist, produced many drawings and prints based upon his experiences with the corps. Several of them appear in this book. As many as fifty-one men, including Lewis and Clark, set out on the expedition, and seven additional people joined after the journey was under way.

were separated into three squads, each reporting to a sergeant. Clark's slave, York, was also on the trip but is not listed on the official roster.

To ensure that the corps would be able to communicate with the Native Americans they met on the trip, Lewis and Clark also hired interpreters fluent in several European and Native American languages. The first was George Drouillard, a skilled hunter, who was able to converse in French, English, and American Indian sign language. Another was Private Pierre Cruzatte, a man who could speak the Omaha Indian language and American Indian sign language. Both Drouillard and Cruzatte were sons of French Canadian fathers and Native American mothers. The last addition to the crew was Seaman, a big

Newfoundland dog that was brought along as a companion and to help with the hunting.

Once the boats were ready, Lewis took off down the Ohio River on August 30, 1803, heading for the Mississippi to eventually meet up with Clark and the men—the group of explorers and adventurers who would become known as the Corps of Discovery. On this initial trip to Clarksville with eleven men and the dog, Seaman, Lewis made his first entry in a journal that would provide future generations with an incredible record of this great American adventure.

After picking up Clark and the remaining members of the corps in mid-October, the group sailed on to St. Louis, reaching it in December 1803. The corps established its winter camp on the east side of the Mississippi, at River Dubois in Illinois Territory, just across from the meeting of the Missouri and Mississippi Rivers. The rest of the winter and following spring were spent making last-minute arrangements, recruiting for remaining spots in the corps, drilling corps members in army tactics and techniques, and receiving and packing supplies and equipment.

Finally, on May 14, 1804, after months of painstaking preparation and years of planning, the Corps of Discovery set off on its mission. Clark, the men, and the supplies started up the Missouri River in the keelboat and two dugout canoes called pirogues. In two days, they reached St. Charles, where Lewis would join them a few days later. Everything was ready at last. It was time for the Corps of Discovery to begin its expedition!

CHAPTER 2

UP THE MISSOURI

The Corps of Discovery officially embarked on its momentous journey from the Missouri River town of St. Charles on May 21, 1804, at about four o'clock in the afternoon. There was no parade, flowery speeches, or public celebration to mark their departure. Instead, they simply shoved off and quietly began rowing up the Missouri River while a few interested locals stood on the riverbank and gave them three cheers. The keelboat and pirogues were filled with supplies and almost forty men.

Agony and Awe

From the beginning, the trip was not a smooth one. The Missouri River was not easy to navigate. Sandbars, driftwood, and sunken logs were hazards that frequently made the boats either run aground or become snagged. Some sections of the river had rushing currents, while others had still, shallow waters. The men were further tested by everything from severe thunderstorms

This painting commissioned by the Missouri Banker's Association depicts the May 21, 1804, departure of the Corps of Discovery from the banks of the Missouri River in St. Charles, Missouri. In William Clark's notebook sketch *(below)*, the keelboat is seen from the top and side. The boat could be rowed by twenty men, ten on each side. The side view shows the boat's mast upon which a large sail was furled. Generally, however, the boat was rowed or pulled with tow ropes by men walking along the shore.

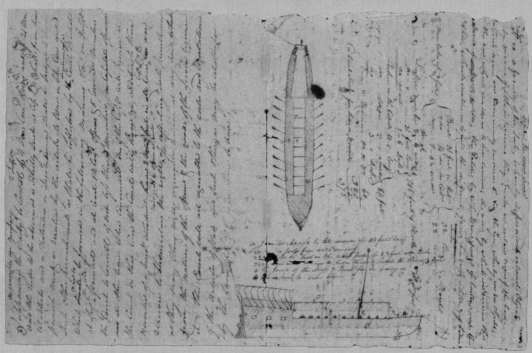

and swarms of mosquitoes and ticks to bouts of diarrhea and cases of sunstroke. Infections were common. One man, Sergeant Charles Floyd, died near present-day Sioux City, Iowa, from appendicitis (a sometimes deadly swelling and bursting of the appendix, a narrow tube in the lower right portion of the abdomen). He became the first U.S. soldier in the nation's history to die west of the Mississippi.

The boats averaged ten to fifteen miles a day. With a strong, steady wind behind them, they could use their sails and cover more than twenty miles. A still day, on the other hand, might mean they could travel only five or six miles. Clark was the better river man, so he stayed on the boats to help navigate and manage the men. Lewis would often remain on land and walk along the shoreline, taking extensive notes on what he saw and collecting soil samples.

One of Lewis's main duties was to report back to Jefferson on the unusual plants and animals he encountered during the journey. Sometimes he would simply sketch what he observed in his journal, adding to the drawing informative notes and observations. Other times, he collected actual samples and wrote descriptions that he would later have shipped back to Jefferson.

A number of animals were observed on this portion of the trip that amazed and baffled the men. Many of them were caught, weighed, measured, and dissected so that all the details

One of Clark's journals, bound in elkskin *(bottom)*. Above, a March 1806 sketch by William Clark of a sage grouse with an accompanying description. Corps members sketched various examples of plant and animal life accompanied by their descriptions and observations. In the course of their expedition, the Corps of Discovery recorded 178 plants and 122 animals not previously known to exist. See transcript on page 58.

of each newly discovered species could be faithfully reported to the president. The members of the corps were especially fascinated by prairie dogs, or what they called "barking dogs." After many failed attempts, they eventually succeeded in capturing one. Along the course of the two-year journey, they also discovered coyotes, jackrabbits, buffalo, mule deer, and antelopes. In all, the Corps of Discovery recorded an amazing 178 plants, 122 animals, and 40 Native American tribes that had previously been unknown to white settlers of the United States.

Making Camp

At the end of an exhausting day, the men would turn the boats to shore and make camp along the riverbank. Each of the three groups that constituted the corps was assigned a job, from preparing food and hunting to setting up tents and gathering firewood. Cruzatte might entertain everyone by playing the fiddle, while others were sent out to hunt for something to supplement the usual diet of cornmeal and lard or pork and flour.

When hunting was good, the men ate as much as eight pounds of meat a day. This impressive intake was no doubt necessary to help maintain their energy for the demanding work of the long, exhausting expedition. Hunters would often return with game ranging from turkey and geese to bear and elk. Roasted beaver tail was considered a delicacy. Some of the meat was dried into a jerky-like treat and carried in the men's pockets for midday snacking.

During the course of the evening, some of the men, including Lewis and Clark, would take out journals that they were keeping. President Jefferson had insisted that the men keep detailed records. Lewis asked each one of his sergeants to keep a separate daily journal to record the important events of the expedition and noteworthy observations about the land, the people, and the animals they encountered. Ironically, the one person who had significant lapses in his diary was Lewis himself.

Native American Encounters

As the expedition proceeded upriver and the men continued to record their awed observations of the new lands, the captains began to feel a growing anxiety about what they had not yet observed—Native Americans. More than two months after the corps had sailed past La Charette, the last white settlement along the Missouri River on May 25, 1804, they still had not encountered a single Native American.

In early August, this changed. Camped at the junction of the Missouri and Platte Rivers, about one hundred miles past the southern border of present-day Iowa, the group was startled when fourteen Oto and Missouri Indians suddenly appeared in their camp. Fortunately, this tribe was friendly. Soon, an exchange of food was made and a meeting was set up for the following day.

All the men of the corps appeared at the meeting in dress uniform to impress the Native Americans. Lewis carefully explained to the Oto and Missouri how the territory no longer belonged to France or Spain but was now part of the United States. As he handed out the peace medals, he explained that President Jefferson was now the Native Americans' "Great White Father."

The events of this first meeting between the corps and an American Indian tribe were repeated in many future encounters with other American Indian nations. In most meetings, Lewis and Clark explained to tribal leaders that their land now belonged to the United States and that President Jefferson was

This is an 1832 painting by George Catlin of an elderly Hidatsa chief named Eh-Toh'K-Pah-She-Pee-Shah, also known as "Black Moccasin." He was a village leader in the Awatixa (Hidatsa) community called Metaharta, where Sacagawea and Charbonneau were living when Lewis and Clark first met them. When Catlin visited the village in 1832, Black Moccasin was one of the only Hidatsa still alive who had known Lewis and Clark.

their new Great White Father. Then the peace medals were handed out along with fifteen-star American flags and other gifts. Often a military parade followed, with uniformed corps members marching and firing their guns. The corps tried to impress the Native Americans with their technological gadgets, such as compasses, telescopes, and magnets. Finally, Lewis and Clark promised the tribes that a future of peace and prosperity through trade was theirs if they refrained from attacking white settlers and other tribes.

Autumn's Arrival

The signs were all around them. Leaves were changing color and dropping from the trees. The days were getting shorter. Flocks of birds were seen overhead heading south. Autumn had arrived, and that meant that winter would follow close behind. The corps was near the present-day border between South Dakota and North Dakota when they encountered the Arikara Indians. These Indians were gentle farmers who became fascinated by Clark's African American slave, York. Having never seen black skin before, they touched him with awe, wetting their fingers to see if the darkness would rub off.

The captains knew that travel during the winter would be even more difficult than it had already been. Settling in somewhere for the harsh, cold months ahead seemed to be a wise choice. Late in October, the first snowflakes were spotted. On October 24, 1804, the corps, with the Arikara chief serving as goodwill ambassador, reached the villages of the Mandan and Hidatsa tribes, large settlements north of present-day Bismarck, North Dakota, whose population exceeded those of St. Louis or Washington, D.C., at the time.

The Corps of Discovery spent the winter of 1804–1805 with the Mandan Indians, who lived along the upper Missouri River in present-day central North Dakota. The Mandan lived in two villages—Matootonha on the western bank of the Missouri and, farther north, Rooptahee on the eastern bank. The corps built a fort across the river from Matootonha and named it Fort Mandan in tribute to their friendly and generous hosts. In this 1833–1834 painting by Karl Bodmer, entitled *Mih-Tutta-Hang-Kusch, Mandan Village*, the Mandan are seen crossing the frozen Missouri.

Like the Arikara, the Mandan and Hidatsa were friendly farmers who welcomed the corps to their villages. Lewis and Clark decided to stay the winter with them and built a series of cabins from cottonwood logs. They finished the temporary settlement, naming it Fort Mandan, and had moved in by Christmas Eve. The corps raised the U.S. flag over the fort just in time for winter to begin blowing full force. For now, the expedition was on hold until weather made it possible for them to move upriver once again.

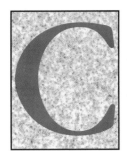

CHAPTER 3

The winter was a long, cold, and rather boring one for the men of the Corps of Discovery. They were snowed in for more than four months, and temperatures often dropped to -45°F (-43°C). Despite this, the men were still expected to maintain military discipline by performing daily drills and serving on guard duty.

Sacagawea

In November, a French Canadian fur trader who lived among the Hidatsa, Toussaint Charbonneau, paid a visit to Lewis and Clark.

INTO THE WEST

He hoped to join the expedition as an interpreter and bring along his pregnant young wife, Sacagawea, a Shoshone Indian who had been captured by the Hidatsa five years earlier and sold to Charbonneau. The captains hired Charbonneau for his skills as an interpreter, but they felt that Sacagawea would be most useful to the expedition. Her presence on the trip would assure many of the Native American tribes they encountered that they were a peaceful group, not a war party. In addition, the Shoshone tribe, who lived at the headwaters of the Missouri River near the Continental Divide in the Rocky Mountains, had many horses. Sacagawea could help the corps in their attempts to buy horses from the Shoshone.

On February 11, 1805, Sacagawea gave birth to a son, who was named Jean-Baptiste Charbonneau. He quickly acquired the

This 1837 painting by Alfred Jacob Miller, entitled *The Trapper's Bride*, depicts a wedding ceremony that may have been very similar to that of the Shoshone Indian Sacagawea and Toussaint Charbonneau, a French Canadian fur trader. It was not at all uncommon for European fur traders to purchase and marry one or even two Indian women, just as Charbonneau had done. Both Charbonneau and Sacagawea were hired by the corps as translators, but Sacagawea would also prove to be a valuable intermediary between the corps and other Indian tribes.

nickname of Pomp, however. Lewis assisted in the birth and tried to speed the delivery and ease Sacagawea's pain by offering her a potion that included the powder of a crushed rattle from a rattlesnake.

Gathering Information

During the corps' time at Fort Mandan, Lewis and Clark received valuable information from the Native Americans about the surrounding area and the terrain the corps would encounter once they departed in the spring. Through sign language and drawings, the men learned that they would be facing waterfalls and mountains soon. Throughout the winter, Clark worked on a map of the area between the upper Mississippi and Missouri Rivers and the major tributaries of the lower and middle Missouri. This map was based on his own observations and his conversations with Native Americans and traders.

The captains spent most of the winter months putting together information, specimens, and artifacts that could be sent back to Jefferson as soon as the river thawed. In early April 1805, Lewis and Clark loaded the keelboat, which was too clumsy to navigate the upcoming waters, with five boxes of maps, sketches, reports, soil and plant specimens, mineral samples, charts, animal skins and skeletons, horns, Native American gifts, live magpies, and even a caged prairie dog! Twelve men from the corps accompanied the boat back to St. Louis.

Uncharted Territory

On April 7, 1805, the same day that the keelboat was sent on its way back to St. Louis, Lewis, Clark, and thirty-one remaining members of the corps (including Charbonneau, Sacagawea, and Jean-Baptiste) set off in the opposite direction in six small canoes and the two pirogues. According to PBS Online, Lewis wrote of this departure in his journal: "We were now about to penetrate a country at least two thousand miles in width, on which the foot of civilized man had never trodden ... I could but esteem this moment of my departure as among the most happy of my life."

The rowing was difficult. They were traveling against the Missouri's current, and the crew was plagued by cold winds, smoke from prairie grass fires, and hordes of mosquitoes. Often the men would be blistered by the sun from the waist up, while from the waist down they were submerged in icy cold water, as

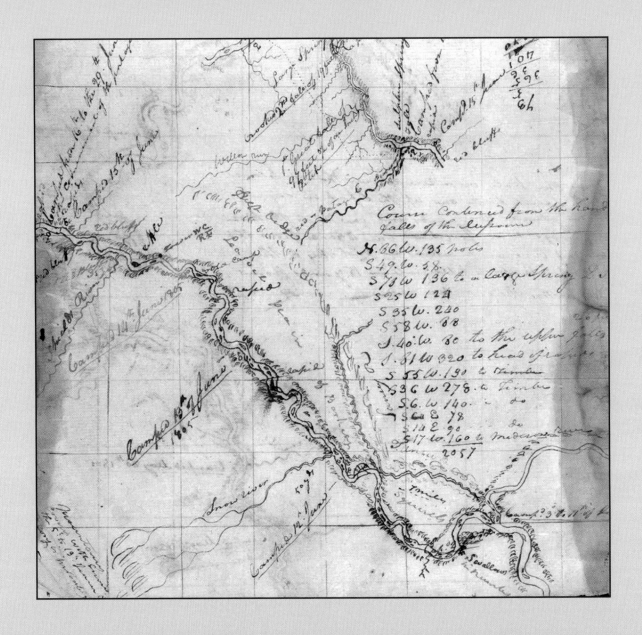

This is William Clark's sketched map of the fork in the Missouri River *(lower right-hand corner)* that confused the Corps of Discovery and required a week of scouting trips to determine the correct branch to take to continue the westward journey. Lewis became convinced that the left fork would lead them to the great waterfall described to him by the Hidatsa Indians. His hunch proved to be correct. Lewis named the right fork the Marias River, after a cousin in Virginia.

they carried or dragged the boats through shallow streams and rocky patches. By the end of April, the corps had entered present-day Montana, farther west than any known white person had ever traveled on the Missouri River.

As the journey upriver progressed, however, group spirits lifted. There was plenty of game in this area, so food was abundant, and the weather continued to improve each day. Herds of buffalo numbering several thousand were not uncommon. It is estimated that members of the corps were eating as much as ten pounds of buffalo meat a day during this portion of the journey. A serious challenge was waiting ahead for the captains, however, and it was one that could mean weeks of delay if they made the wrong choice.

The Great Falls

Up to this point, Lewis and Clark had been following the information the Hidatsa had given them about the terrain. On June 2, 1805, the corps was suddenly faced with an unexpected choice and a difficult decision. The Missouri River forked, with one stream appearing to run southwest and the other northwest. Which one was the "true" Missouri? Both forks seemed to be roughly the same size, offering no visual clue as to which one should be followed.

Traveling slightly ahead of the corps, Lewis and a few others journeyed down the south fork to see if they could find the waterfalls that the Hidatsa had told them about. If they found the waterfalls, they would know they had chosen the correct path. Two days after setting out, the advance party found the waterfalls, which Lewis considered to be the grandest sight he had ever beheld.

On June 13, 1805, the Corps of Discovery reached the Great Falls *(top)* in present-day Montana. The tallest of the five falls rose ninety feet above the awed men. Fast-running water posed many perils for the corps members, including the capsizing of canoes, as depicted in this 1812 Patrick Gass print *(bottom)*. In addition to jeopardizing corps members' lives, capsized boats also threatened the maps, journals, and artifacts collected by Lewis and Clark.

Although the falls were beautiful, they definitely presented a problem for the Corps of Discovery. The Great Falls, as Lewis christened them, were not a single waterfall, but a network of five falls stretching out over more than ten miles of river. Since the corps would not be able to navigate this dangerous stretch of river, Lewis and Clark needed to find a way around the falls. That meant carrying the boats and supplies over eighteen and a half miles of land.

The crew's strength and endurance were severely tested during this period of the trip. Before they could transport their supplies, cargo, and boats across the land, they first had to cut down miles of undergrowth (low plants, shrubs, and trees) that blocked or slowed their way. Wheels needed to be made for the boats, and wagons had to be built to carry the supplies. Once the corps was finally able to start moving, they were attacked by mosquitoes, menaced by rattlesnakes, blistered by heat, pricked by cacti, and pelted with apple-sized hailstones during a storm. A flash flood almost drowned Sacagawea, Charbonneau, Clark, and York. It took almost a month to get around the Great Falls and reach a stretch of the Missouri River that was safe to navigate.

By mid-July, the group was back on the river. Soon after, they entered a three-mile-long gorge of immense proportions. Cliffs rose on each side of the water to heights of more than fourteen hundred feet, and there was no shoreline to set camp. Lewis christened the place the Gates of the Rocky Mountains. Hoping to discover the fabled Northwest Passage to the Pacific Ocean on the other side of this "gate," Lewis had little idea of the might, majesty, and extent of the mountains that stretched out far beyond his immediate sight.

CHAPTER 4

A BITTER CLIMB, A SWEET SUCCESS

The Corps of Discovery was getting worried. In June 1805, the men first spotted the tops of the snowy mountains that were still far away but stretched as far as the eye could see. They reluctantly accepted that there was no Northwest Passage that would take them through or around these mountains to reach the Pacific Ocean on the other side. Instead, they would have to climb over them.

Sacagawea's Homecoming

The trip from the Missouri River up over the Rockies and down to the Columbia River (which empties into the Pacific) was going to be an incredibly difficult one, and it would have to be done on land. It was almost time to abandon the boats and go back to riding horses. The problem was they did not have any horses. Their only hope of getting any rested with the Shoshone Indians, who, so far, had not been seen.

Clark, York, Sacagawea, and a few other corps members headed off to search for some Shoshone. Sacagawea began to recognize landmarks from the childhood years she had spent in the area before she had been taken away from her people. She suspected that they were close to the country of her ancestors. On August 11, 1805, traveling ahead of the corps, Lewis and three men sighted a Shoshone scout on horseback, but he rode off before they could talk to him and declare their peaceful intentions.

Two days later, Lewis came across three Native American women. Although they initially thought he meant to hurt them, he quickly offered them gifts, and they realized he was not dangerous. He was led back to their village and was accepted with embraces and smiles. When the rest of the corps was brought to the tribe to begin negotiating for horses, a wonderful surprise awaited all assembled. The chief of the Shoshone, Cameahwait, turned out to be Sacagawea's brother. There were many tears and much rejoicing by everyone who witnessed the unexpected family reunion.

After this joyous wave of emotion subsided, however, it was time to get down to business. Convincing the Shoshone, a poor tribe, to trade horses for knives, trinkets, tobacco, mirrors, and ammunition was not easy. In the end, however, the corps was able to obtain twenty-nine horses and a mule for the trip. Cameahwait warned the men that crossing in autumn would be dangerous and the game scarce, but the men could not be persuaded to wait for spring. They needed to move on.

Mountains of Misery

The crossing of the Rockies would prove to be the most difficult and treacherous part of the entire journey. Guided by an elderly Shoshone they nicknamed Old Toby, the captains and their crew headed out for the Bitterroot Mountains of Idaho. In the coming days, they encountered so much misery they almost could not go on. They ran out of food and had to shoot and eat three of the horses. Each day brought an awful combination of rain, sleet, and snow. The men were cold, hungry, and wet all the time. The climbing was steep and slippery. They occasionally lost the trail.

The dramatic moment when Meriwether Lewis caught his first glimpse of the majestic Rocky Mountains is depicted in this Olaf Seltzer painting entitled *Lewis' First Glimpse of the Rockies*. Lewis believed that the mountain chain would be narrow and that it could be quickly crossed. On the other side he expected to see the Columbia River winding along a plain that would quickly lead to the Pacific Ocean. Instead, for the next three months, the Corps of Discovery saw nothing but mountains, spreading out before them to the horizon line.

Even after two weeks of exhausting effort, mountains continued to stretch west as far their eyes could see. The Rockies were far more extensive than they had believed, and the Pacific Ocean still seemed impossibly distant and difficult to reach.

On September 17, 1805, the corps, on the brink of starvation, met and discussed their chances of survival and possible strategies. They were simply too tired to go back, so they kept going forward.

On September 22, the corps finally emerged from the Bitterroot Mountains near present-day Weippe, Idaho, thirteen days after they began their ascent, and soon stumbled upon a Nez Percé (French for "pierced nose") Indian village. Fortunately for the weakened and dejected corps, this was a friendly and welcoming tribe. Lewis, Clark, and the rest of the crew stayed in the Nez Percé camp for a week, recovering from starvation and exhaustion and feasting on salmon. They built five new canoes from hollowed-out pine trees and left their horses with Chief Twisted Hair for safekeeping.

By the end of the first week of October, they were on the move again, this time on the Clearwater River. These waters were full of rapids, and for once, the corps was going with the current. Their progress was very swift, and food was plentiful since the entire river was full of salmon. The men lived on these fish—and became terribly tired of it, too. Happily, though, the Clearwater River led to the Snake River, which in turn emptied into the Columbia River. They were quickly drawing closer to the Pacific Ocean.

The corps, having been away from home for two years, was so eager to reach their final westward destination that they misjudged where the ocean was. On November 7, Clark wrote in his journal (as quoted in George Sullivan's *Lewis and Clark: In Their Own Words*), "Ocian in view! O! the joy! . . . Great joy in the camp we are in View of the Ocian, this great Pacific Ocean which we been So long anxious to see." Unfortunately, the men were mistaken. The large body of water before them was only Gray's Bay, a widening in the Columbia River. Their long-sought goal, however, lay only twenty miles away.

Land's End

Because of stormy weather, it would take almost three weeks for the corps to finally reach the ocean. When they did, they were too tired to celebrate. They were exhausted, hungry, wet, and ready to rest. Having traveled more than four thousand miles from the mouth of the Missouri River to the Pacific Ocean, they needed to regain their strength and energy for the long return journey.

Even though their goal had been reached, the corps still had a big decision to make. Should they head back to St. Louis immediately or wait until the winter was over? Taking a vote, which included Clark's slave, York, and Sacagawea, the group decided to spend the winter on the south side of the Columbia River, near present-day Astoria, Oregon. Immediately, they began to build a log fort, which they named Fort Clatsop after the Native American tribe nearby.

Once again, it was a long and dreary winter. While there was less snow in this area of the country, there was almost constant rain. That winter Lewis reported that there were only twelve days without rain. The dampness was so extreme that clothes mildewed and food rotted quickly. Corps members passed the time by making three hundred pairs of moccasins, as well as new shirts and trousers to replace what had been destroyed by the humidity. The men could not wait for winter to end. The arrival of spring meant only one thing to them: It was time to go home!

CHAPTER 5

On March 23, 1806, the journey began that would take the Corps of Discovery back home. They were determined to reach St. Louis before yet another winter had time to set in. Traveling up the Columbia River was a true challenge because the powerful current was against them and the rapids were vicious. Eventually, the corps decided to burn the canoes and make the trip on foot. By early May, they had reached the Nez Percé village they had visited the previous autumn where their horses were waiting for them.

A JOURNEY'S END AND A NATION'S NEW BEGINNING

Lewis and Clark wanted to continue east immediately, but they had to wait two weeks for deep snow on the Bitterroot Mountains to melt. Finally, with three Nez Percé guides to help them, they began the long trip home. The going was tough, but on June 30, they emerged from the mountains with the knowledge that, from this point forward, the trip would only get easier.

On August 14, the corps passed through the Mandan camp where they had wintered almost two years earlier. As they passed through, they said good-bye to Sacagawea, Charbonneau,

This October 29, 1806, article from Boston's *Columbian Centinel* announces the return of Captains Lewis and Clark from their western expedition. Because the telegraph (much less the telephone, fax, or Internet) had not yet been invented, news traveled extremely slowly. This story appeared almost five weeks after the Corps of Discovery arrived in St. Louis on September 23, 1806. See transcript on page 58.

and Jean-Baptiste, who stayed behind. This was not their last contact, however. In later years, Jean-Baptiste would become an adopted member of Clark's family. Although the Charbonneaus stayed behind, the Mandan chief, Sheheke ("Coyote," also called "Big White"), and his wife Yellow Corn traveled to St. Louis with the captains.

By September, the corps had returned to the Missouri River and were covering seventy miles a day on its swift current. On September 23, 1806, Lewis and Clark and their crew arrived in St. Louis. People there were shocked to find that the men were still alive. It had been so long since anyone had received any word of the expedition that they had feared the worse.

Although the expedition had received almost no attention when it set out, the members of the corps became national heroes upon their return. Banquets, balls, parades, and gun salutes were held in their honor. Congress awarded all the group's members double pay ($8 per month, or $224 total) and 320 acres of land. Lewis was paid $40 for each month he was gone (approximately $1,128 total), as well as 1,600 acres. Clark received $30 a month ($840 total) and 1,600 acres.

This portrait of Meriwether Lewis by the French artist Charles B. J. F. de Saint-Memin was made soon after the expedition's completion and Lewis's triumphant return to Washington, D.C. He is shown wearing a tippet—a fur cape made of otter fur and more than a hundred white weasel skins. This cape was probably given to him by the Shoshone, possibly by Chief Cameahwait, Sacagawea's brother. Lewis's final years were marked by severe depression, and he committed suicide in 1809, three years to the month after his return from the western expedition.

Life After the Corps

After the incredible journey was over and life began to settle down, Lewis and Clark found themselves going in different directions. Lewis was appointed the governor of the Territory of Upper Louisiana in 1807, but he never enjoyed the job. He seemed to fall into depression and began to drink heavily. In September 1809, on his way to Washington, D.C., to report on the state of affairs in the Louisiana Territory, Lewis apparently committed suicide in Tennessee by shooting himself in the head and chest. Some people believed he was murdered, but his closest friends, Clark and Jefferson, both believed he killed himself.

This 1830 George Catlin portrait shows an elderly William Clark twenty-four years after his return from the western expedition that shaped and transformed his life. In 1807, Thomas Jefferson appointed him principal Indian agent for the Louisiana Territory and brigadier general of its militia. Until his death in 1838, Clark would continue to serve Missouri, as governor of the territory and super-intendent of Indian Affairs after Missouri became a state. From his first encounters with Indians on the western expedition to his last days in St. Louis, Clark was viewed by many Indians as a fair and honest man.

Clark, on the other hand, followed a far more prosperous path. In January 1807, he was made brigadier general of the Louisiana Militia and superintendent of Indian Affairs for the territory of Upper Louisiana. On January 5, 1808, he married Julia Hancock. They would have five children together. In 1813, Clark became governor of the Missouri Territory, a position he held until Missouri became a state in 1820. He continued to serve as superintendent of Indian Affairs and, over the years, earned the respect of many Native Americans. They often provided him with new information about western lands that allowed him to continuously update his map of the American West. Clark lived a full and happy life, dying in 1838 at the age of sixty-eight.

Most historical accounts report that Sacagawea passed away in 1812 in South Dakota. Others believe that she lived to be more than one hundred years old and died on a reservation in Wyoming. Her son, Jean-Baptiste, was raised from the age of six by Clark and his family, eventually being adopted by them. Charbonneau lived to his early eighties. Perhaps Jean-Baptiste's parents wished to offer him an education and the chance to lead a prosperous life.

The information the Corps of Discovery returned with would change the course of history. Even though they had to report the disappointing news that there was no all-water passage linking the Atlantic and Pacific Oceans, the trip was still considered a tremendous success. Lewis and Clark's extraordinarily courageous expedition had a profound effect on the future of America's development. The expedition provided the knowledge that would make western travel and settlement a reality. It detailed the territory's natural bounty, resulting in fur trading becoming a hugely profitable business. Eastern goods found new markets as trade routes opened and the population spread westward, providing the national economy with an enormous boost. Finally, Lewis and

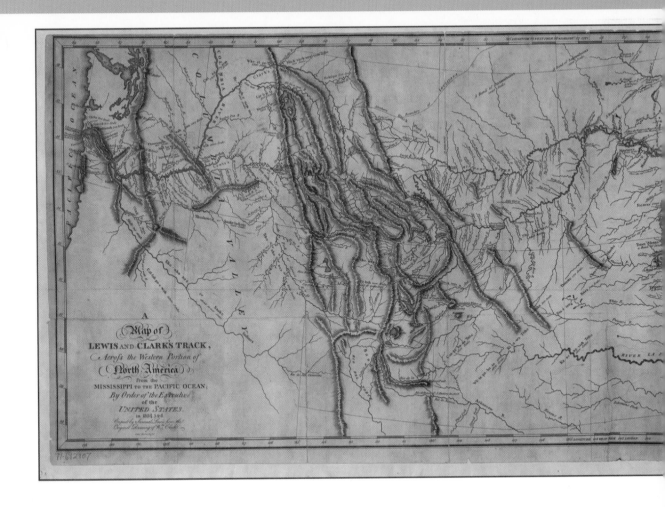

Clark's expedition helped to establish the United States's claim to the Louisiana Territory, allowing the country to obtain even more land—such as the Oregon Territory—and further reduce the European presence and influence in North America.

The Corps of Discovery's two and a half years in the wilderness set the stage for great transformation: a tiny, immature collection of former colonies surrounded by scheming European powers would soon turn into an enormous, influential, independent, and wealthy nation prepared to take its place on the world stage. The courage, determination, and resilience of Lewis and Clark's Corps of Discovery proved to the young country that new land awaited them, full of delightful discoveries, awe-inspiring

This map of the American West, first begun by William Clark at Fort Clatsop during the winter of 1805–1806, is perhaps the greatest legacy of the Lewis and Clark expedition. Based on Clark's daily compass readings, the 4-foot wide (1.2 meters) map provided the most detailed depiction of the rivers, plains, mountains, and lakes west of the Mississippi recorded to that point. The information it provided encouraged new settlement and trade opportunities and opened American eyes to the rich possibilities of their newly acquired western lands. Clark's map was the first graphic symbol of a United States that stretched from sea to shining sea.

sights, abundant adventures, untold riches, and limitless opportunities. The corps' fantastic journey first introduced Americans to the land they would come to call their own. It expanded the American imagination and sense of destiny as it enlarged the country's borders. The members of the Corps of Discovery emerged from the wilderness into a country that would soon change drastically as a result of their courageous exploration.

Page 10: President Thomas Jefferson's Confidential Message to Congress Regarding Indian Relations and the Proposed Lewis and Clark Expedition, January 18, 1803

Transcription

The river Missouri, and the Indians inhabiting it, are not as well known as is rendered desirable by their connexion with the Mississippi, and consequently with us. It is, however, understood, that the country on that river is inhabited by numerous tribes, who furnish great supplies of furs and peltry to the trade of another nation, carried on in a high latitude, through an infinite number of portages and lakes, shut up by ice through a long season. The commerce on that line could bear no competition with that of the Missouri, traversing a moderate climate, offering according to the best accounts, a continued navigation from its source, and possibly with a single portage, from the Western Ocean, and finding to the Atlantic a choice of channels through the Illinois or Wabash, the lakes and Hudson, through the Ohio and Susquehanna, or Potomac or James rivers, and through the Tennessee and Savannah, rivers. An intelligent officer, with ten or twelve chosen men, fit for the enterprise, and willing to undertake it, taken from our posts, where they may be spared without inconvenience, might explore the whole line, even to the Western Ocean, have conferences with the natives on the subject of commercial intercourse, get admission among them for our traders, as others are admitted, agree on convenient deposits for an interchange of articles, and return with the information acquired, in the course of two summers. Their arms and accoutrements, some instruments of observation, and light and cheap presents for the Indians, would be all the apparatus they could carry, and with an expectation of a soldier's portion of land on their return, would constitute the whole expense. Their pay would be going on, whether here or there. While other civilized nations have encountered great expense to enlarge the boundaries of knowledge by undertaking voyages of discovery, and for other literary purposes, in various parts and directions, our nation seems to owe to the same object, as well as to its own interests, to explore this, the only line of easy communication across the continent, and so directly traversing our own part of it. The interests of commerce place the principal object within the constitutional powers and care of Congress, and that it should incidentally advance the geographical knowledge of our own continent, cannot be but an additional gratification. The nation claiming the territory, regarding this as a literary pursuit, which is in the habit of permitting within its dominions, would not be disposed to view it with jealousy, even if the expiring state of its interests there did not render it a matter of indifference. The appropriation of two thousand five hundred dollars, "for the purpose of extending the external commerce of the United States," while understood and considered by the Executive as giving the legislative sanction, would cover the undertaking from notice, and prevent the obstructions which interested individuals might otherwise previously prepare in its way.

TH. Jefferson
Jan. 18. 1803.

Contemporary English Translation

We are not as familiar with the Indians living along the Missouri River as we should be, given that they live so close to the Mississippi [the U.S.'s current western border and economic lifeline]. We do know, however, that many tribes live along the Missouri. Using a large network of lakes and land crossings, they send a lot of furs and pelts far up north—where severe weather and icy conditions make the trading season short—to traders of another country. It's possible that we could take over this fur trade by taking advantage of the Missouri area's mild climate and the river's likely direct route to the Pacific Ocean. Goods brought out of the West along the Missouri could then be sent East to the Atlantic Ocean through any of a number of river and lake passages. A smart officer with ten or twelve trusted, handpicked soldiers who could be spared from our forts and were physically and mentally up to the challenge could explore the whole length of the Missouri River system, maybe even all the way to the Pacific. They could also meet with Indian tribes and begin discussing trade opportunities and agreements. Within two years, the expedition would return armed with new information on the western lands, the river, the Indians, and trade arrangements. The soldiers would carry only some guns, some scientific equipment, and cheap presents for the Indians. When they returned, each corps member would receive the standard plot of land offered to soldiers. These items would be the expedition's only expense. Since the corps members will be drawn from the military, we will have to pay these soldiers whether they go on the expedition or stay behind, so their salary is no extra expense. Other nations have spent a lot of money to organize voyages to explore the unknown. We owe it to our country to explore this continent and to try to find the most direct route across it. Since the discovery of a direct cross-country route would have a huge economic value, it is Congress's right to organize an expedition to explore the West. Any geographical knowledge we would gain as a result would be an added bonus. The economic motive for the expedition could be disguised so that the country that currently claims the territory [France] would not feel threatened (even though they shouldn't get angry since their ownership of the land is about to be transferred to us). If you allow only $2,500 to be spent on the expedition, for the stated purpose of developing new trade opportunities, few people will take notice of the project and there will be few objections to it.

T.H. Jefferson
Jan. 18. 1803.

Page 21: Meriwether Lewis's List of Provisions Needed for the Corps of Discovery's Expedition, c. 1803

Transcription

Arms & Accoutrements
15 Rifles
15 Powder Horns & pouches complete
15 Pairs of Bullet Moulds
15 do. [dozen] Of Wipers or Gun worms
15 Ball Screws
24 Pipe Tomahawks
24 large knives
Extra parts of Locks & tools for repairing arms
15 Gun Slings
500 best Flints

Ammunition
200 lbs. [pounds] Best rifle powder
400 lbs. Lead

Clothing
15 3 pt. [point] Blankets
15 Watch Coats with Hoods & belts
15 Woolen Overalls
15 Rifle Frocks of waterproof Cloth if possible
30 Pairs of Socks or half Stockings
20 Fatigue Frocks or hinting shirts
30 Shirts of Strong linnen
30 yds. [yards] Common flannel.

Page 31: William Clark's Description of the "Cock of the Plain" (Sage Grouse) in a Journal Entry, c. March 1806

Transcription

Grouse The feathers about its head are pointed and stiff. Some hairs [?] about the base of the beak. Feathers short fine and stiff about the ears, and eye. This is a faint likenefs [likeness] of the Cock of the Plains or Heath Cock. The first of these fowls which we met with was on the Mifsouri [Missouri] below and in the neighborhood of the Rocky Mountains and from to the Mountain which pafs [?; pass?] the Columbia between the Great Falls and Rapids. They go in large gangues [gangs?] or singularly and hide hide remarkably close when pursued, make short flights, etc. The large Black & White Pheasant is peculiar to that of the Rocky Mountains watered by the Columbia River. At least we did not see them until we reached the waters of that river, nor since we have left those mountains. They are about the size of a well grown hen. The contour of the bird is much that of the reddish brown Pheasant common to our country.

Page 50: An October 29, 1806, *Columbian Centinel* (Boston, MA) Newspaper Article Announcing the Return of the Corps of Discovery to St. Louis on September 23, 1806

Transcription

By the last Mails.
MARYLAND. BALTIMORE, Oct. 29, 1806.
A Letter from St. Louis (Upper Louifiana) [Upper Louisiana], dated Sept. 23, 1806, announces the arrival of Captains LEWIS and CLARK, from their expedition into the interior.—They went to the Pacific Ocean; have brought fome [some] of the natives and curiofities [curiosities] of the countries through which they paffed [passed], and only loft [lost] one man. They left the Pacific Ocean 23d March, 1806, where they arrived in November, 1805;—and where fome [some] American veffels [vessels] had been juft [just] before.—They ftate [state] the Indians to be as numerous on the Columbia river, which empties into the Pacific, as the whites in any part of the U.S. They brought a family of the Mandan indians with them. The winter was very mild on the Pacific.—They have kept an ample journal of their tour; which will be publifhed [published] and muft [must] afford much intelligence.

GLOSSARY

appendicitis Inflammation of the appendix (a small internal organ located in the lower right portion of the abdomen).

astronomy The study of objects and matter outside Earth's atmosphere.

botany The study of plants.

cartography The study and art of making maps.

chronometer An extremely precise timepiece that can be used to help calculate longitude.

counteroffer An offer in response to another offer as part of a negotiating process.

diplomat Someone who conducts negotiations between nations.

encroachment To advance beyond the proper limit.

expedition A journey taken for a specific purpose.

haphazard Random, disorderly.

mineralogy The science and study of minerals and their properties.

naturalist A student of natural history; a biologist.

New World The Western Hemisphere; usually referring to North and South America.

Old World The Eastern Hemisphere, not including Australia; usually referring to Europe.

pirogues Canoes made from hollowed-out tree trunks.

quadrant An instrument used for measuring altitude.

survey To measure the shape, extent, and position of a piece of land.

transcontinental Extending across a continent.

tributary A stream feeding a larger stream or lake.

FOR MORE INFORMATION

Web Sites

Due to the changing nature of Internet links, the Rosen Publishing Group, Inc., has developed an online list of Web sites related to the subject of this book. This site is updated regularly. Please use this link to access the list:

http://www.rosenlinks.com/psah/lecl

FOR FURTHER READING

Fitzgerald, Christine A. *The World's Great Explorers: Meriwether Lewis and William Clark*. Chicago: Children's Press, 1991.

Hall, Eleanor. *The Lewis and Clark Expedition*. San Diego: Lucent Books, 1996.

Herbert, Janis. *Lewis and Clark for Kids: Their Journey of Discovery with 21 Activities*. Chicago: Chicago Review Press, 2000.

Kroll, Steven. *Lewis and Clark: Explorers of the American West*. New York: Holiday House, 1994.

Morley, Jacqueline. *Across America: The Story of Lewis and Clark*. Danbury, CT: Franklin Watts, 1998.

Schanzer, Rosalyn. *How We Crossed the West*. Washington, DC: National Geographic Society, 1997.

Sullivan, George. *Lewis and Clark: In Their Own Words*. New York: Scholastic, 1999.

BIBLIOGRAPHY

Ambrose, Stephen. *Lewis and Clark: Voyage of Discovery*. Washington, DC: National Geographic Society, 1998.

Blumberg, Rhoda. *The Incredible Journey of Lewis and Clark*. New York: Lothrop, Lee, and Shepard Books, 1987.

Cavan, Seamus. *Lewis and Clark and the Route to the Pacific*. Broomall, PA: Chelsea House Publishers, 1991.

Duncan, Dayton, and Ken Burns. *Lewis and Clark: The Journey of the Corps of Discovery*. New York: Alfred Knopf, 1997.

Faber, Harold. *Lewis and Clark: From Ocean to Ocean*. Tarrytown, NY: Benchmark Books, 2002.

Jackson, Donald, ed. *Letters of the Lewis and Clark Expedition with Related Documents*. 2nd ed. Urbana, IL: University of Illinois Press, 1978.

PBS Online. "Lewis & Clark: The Journey of the Corps of Discovery." Retrieved October 2002 (http://www.pbs.org/lewisandclark).

Streissguth, Tom. *Lewis and Clark: Explorers of the Northwest*. Springfield, NJ: Enslow Publishers, 1998.

Sullivan, George. *Lewis and Clark: In Their Own Words*. New York: Scholastic, 1999

Thorp, Daniel. *American Journey: Lewis and Clark*. New York: Metro Books, 1998.

PRIMARY SOURCE IMAGE LIST

Page 5: An 1802 map by Aaron Arrowsmith entitled *A Map Exhibiting All the New Discoveries in the Interior Parts of North America*. Courtesy of the Geography and Map Division of the Library of Congress.

Page 7 (left): An 1805 portrait of Thomas Jefferson by Rembrandt Peale.

Page 7 (right): An 1803 oil on canvas portrait of Napoléon Bonaparte by Francois Gerard. It is housed in the Musee Conde in Chantilly, France. Courtesy of Art Resource.

Page 8: A map entitled *A Map of North America*, 1803, by John Luffman. Housed in the Geography and Map Division of the Library of Congress.

Page 10: An 1803 handwritten document entitled "Jefferson's Confidential Message to Congress Concerning Relations with the Indians, January 18, 1803." Courtesy of the National Archives.

Page 12 (top): A watercolor entitled *View of the West Front of Monticello and Gardens*, 1825, by Jane Braddick Peticolas.

Page 12 (bottom): A buffalo robe probably given to Lewis and Clark by the Mandan and sent to President Thomas Jefferson from Fort Mandan in the spring of 1805. It is now housed in Harvard University's Peabody Museum.

Page 17: An 1807 portrait of Meriwether Lewis by Charles Willson Peale. Courtesy of Independence National Historical Park.

Page 19: An 1807 portrait of William Clark by Charles Willson Peale. Courtesy of Independence National Historic Park.

Page 20: A c. 1803 list of supplies needed for the expedition of the Corps of Discovery, handwritten by Meriwether Lewis. Courtesy of the National Archives.

Page 22 (bottom left): Clark's compass, c. 1803. Courtesy of the Smithsonian Institution.

Page 22 (right): An air rifle made for Meriwether Lewis by Isaiah Lukens, c. 1803. Housed in the Virginia Military Institute Museum.

Page 25 (left): A c. 1821 oil painting entitled *Chiefs of the Lower Missouri*, by Charles Bird King.

Page 26: The roster of men in the Corps of Discovery, handwritten by William Clark, c. 1803. Courtesy of the Beinecke Rare Book and Manuscript Library, Yale Collection of Western Americana.

Page 29 (bottom): A sketch of the Corps of Discovery's keelboat by William Clark that appears in a page of his field notes. Courtesy of the Beinecke Rare Book and Manuscript Library, Yale Collection of Western Americana.

Page 31 (top): A sketch from the journals of William Clark, c. 1806. Courtesy of the Missouri Historical Society.

Page 31 (bottom): One of William Clark's journals bound in elkskin. The page shown here is dated October 26, 1805. Courtesy of the Missouri Historical Society.

Page 34: An 1832 oil painting by George Catlin entitled *Black Moccasin, Aged Chief*. Housed in the Gilcrease Museum, Tulsa, Oklahoma.

Page 36: An 1833–1834 watercolor by Karl Bodmer entitled *Mih-Tutta-Hang-Kusch, Mandan Village*.

Page 38: An 1837 painting entitled *The Trapper's Bride*, by Alfred Jacob Miller.

Page 40: William Clark's draft map of the Missouri River and its fork near the Great Falls, c. June 1805. Courtesy of the Beinecke Rare Book and Manuscript Library, Yale Collection of Western Americana.

Page 42 (top): An engraving entitled *Principal Cascadde of the Missouri*, by W. G. Evans, c. 1842. Courtesy of the Huntington Art Collection, San Marino, California.

Page 42 (bottom): An 1812 engraving by Patrick Gass. The engraving appeared in Gass's *1812 Journal of Voyages and Travels Under Lewis and Clark*. It is housed in the Library of Congress. Courtesy of Corbis.

Page 46: A painting by Olaf Seltzer, entitled *Lewis' First Glimpse of the Rockies*, c. 1830s. Courtesy of the Gilcrease Museum.

Page 50: An October 29, 1806, *Columbian Centinel* (Boston, MA) newspaper article entitled "By the Last Mails," announcing the return of the Corps of Discovery to St. Louis on September 23, 1806. Courtesy of the New York Public Library.

Page 51: A portrait of Meriwether Lewis by Charles B. J. F. de Saint-Memin, c. 1807. Courtesy of the New York Historical Society.

Page 52: An 1830 portrait of William Clark by George Catlin. Housed in the National Portrait Gallery, the Smithsonian Institution.

Pages 54–55: A map entitled *A Map of Lewis and Clark's Track Across the Western Portion of North America From the Mississippi to the Pacific Ocean*, c. 1806, by William Clark. Courtesy of the American Philosophical Society.

INDEX

About the Author

Tamra Orr is a full-time writer living in Portland, Oregon. She is the home-schooling mother of four and has written more than a dozen nonfiction books for children and families. She loves to read, gaze at the mountains, and marvel that Lewis and Clark trekked right through the area she lives in now.

Photo Credits

Front cover, back cover (middle left), pp. 1, 26, 29 (bottom), 40 Yale Collection of Western Americana, Beinecke Rare Book and Manuscript Library; back cover (top left and bottom right), p. 42 (bottom) Library of Congress Prints and Photographs Division; back cover (top right) National Park Service, artist, Keith Rocco; back cover (middle right) Louisiana State Museum, gift of Dr. and Mrs. E. Ralph Lupin; back cover (bottom left) Woolaroc Museum, Bartlesville, Oklahoma; pp. 5, 8, 54–55 Library of Congress Geography and Map Division; pp. 7 (left), 51 Collection of The New-York Historical Society; p. 7 (right) Réunion des Musées Nationaux/Art Resource, NY; pp.10, 21 National Archives and Records Administration; p. 12 (top) Monticello/Thomas Jefferson Foundation, Inc.; p. 12 (bottom) Peabody Museum, Harvard University, T 1908; pp. 17, 19 Independence National Historical Park; p. 22 (top left) Courtesy, Mutter Museum, College of Physicians of Philadelphia; p. 22 (bottom left) National Museum of American History, Smithsonian Institution, Behring Center; p. 22 (right) © VMI Museum, Lexington, Virginia; p. 25 (left) Smithsonian American Art Museum, Washington, DC / Art Resource, NY; p. 25 (right) Courtesy of Oregon Historical Society, Portland (OrHi 101538, OrHi 101540); p. 29 (top) Lewis and Clark, 1804 by L. Edward Fisher, Missouri Bankers Association; p. 31 © North Wind Picture Archives; pp. 34 (George Catlin, Eh-Toh'k-Pah-She-Pee-Shah, The Black Moccasin), 46 (Olaf Seltzer, Lewis' First Glimpse of the Rockies), from the collection of Gilcrease Museum, Tulsa Oklahoma; pp. 36, 38 Joslyn Art Museum, Omaha, Nebraska; p. 42 (top) Reproduced by permission of The Huntington Library, San Marino, California; p. 50 Courtesy of the American Antiquarian Society; p. 52 National Portrait Gallery, Smithsonian Institution/Art Resource, NY.

Designer: Nelson Sá; Photo Researcher: Cindy Reiman